© 2007 Artlist INTERNATIONAL
ISBN: S-TK5-08186-6

THE CAT
Artlist Collection

YOU'RE THE CAT'S MEOW!
How to Love and Raise Your Cat

By The Cats
As told to Sonia Sander

SCHOLASTIC INC.

New York   Toronto   London   Auckland   Sydney
Mexico City   New Delhi   Hong Kong   Buenos Aires

ISBN-13: 978-0-439-02410-5
ISBN-10: 0-439-02410-2

Published by Scholastic Inc. All rights reserved.
SCHOLASTIC and associated logos are trademarks and/or registered trademarks of Scholastic Inc.

10 9 8 7 6 5 4 3   08 09 10 11

Printed in the U.S.A.
First printing, March 2007

Meow!

We cats may act like we don't care if you are there, but you're our guardian, so we care a lot! The truth is, we love everything you do for us. You take over for our mothers. You are the cat's meow!

Are you ready to find out why we need our mothers — both feline and human ones — as much as we do?

Here, Kitty, Kitty!

When our mama cat is ready for us kittens to arrive, she'll need to be as comfortable as possible. She can have three to seven or even more of us in one litter. She won't need much help from you. She will find a quiet, private place all on her own. You should check in every once in a while to make sure the delivery is going smoothly.

Cool Cat Fact

Some cats can find their owner even in a place the cat has never been before.

 Kitty Litter!

Once our mama has delivered all of us kittens, she'll be tired and hungry. Please make sure she is in a warm, quiet place. Line a large box with towels for all of us to lie in. Keep Mama's food and water bowls full and nearby.

Our mama will let you know how much she wants to see you. Too many people or visits might be stressful for our protective mama right after we're born.

Cool Cat Fact

A *kindle* is a group of kittens.
A group of cats is called a *clowder*.

Paws-itively Overprotective!

Don't worry if Mama doesn't let you see us too much at first. She will take very good care of us! Until we are three weeks old, Mama does everything for us herself. Our father usually doesn't help.

From the time we are three weeks old until we are twelve weeks old, our mama teaches us everything we need to know to survive in the world. It's only then that she's ready to let you take over as our mama. But in a big litter of kittens, you can help by watching to make sure that even the smallest one of us gets enough feeding time.

 # Cat Tails!

When we are first born, we are blind. Our eyes are totally closed. It takes a few days before our eyes start to open. It also takes a few days for our ears to start working. Luckily, our mama is there to lick, nuzzle, and guide us to our food. At first we will eat every two to three hours!

Cool Cat Fact

All cats are born with blue eyes.

Cat Got Your Tongue?

When we get to be three weeks old, Mama pushes us to spend more time on our own. We learn how to walk. She lets us explore the world outside our box. But if we stray too far, Mama has a special call to tell us we had better turn back. If she uses that, we know she means business, just like when your mama uses your full name to call you to come inside.

When we're around four weeks old, you can begin to gently cuddle us. That helps us get used to people!

Cool Cat Fact

Our ears can turn 180 degrees. Each ear can also move independently, so we have an extra-sharp sense of hearing!

Smelly Cat!

When we are small, our mother cleans up after us. By the time we're about six weeks old, Mama shows us how to use a litter box. Guess that means a little more cleanup for you! You might want to add another litter box or two, depending on how many of us there are. Sorry about that. Being a mama means doing some dirty work, too. We'll make up for it by snuggling up to you and giving you lots of love.

Cool Cat Fact

If one of us cats blinks at you, it usually means that we love you, or at least that we're relaxed. When we do this, we like you to blink back at us!

Mouse Hunt!

It is about this time that Mama teaches us how to hunt. It doesn't matter if we are indoor or outdoor cats, we still get a lesson if there is prey to hunt. We can be pretty clumsy at this age. Chances are that even if there is a mouse in the house, we won't be able to catch it for another couple of weeks.

Cool Cat Fact

Cats have helped people catch mice for thousands of years. Even way back when, the ancient Egyptians revered their cats above all other animals.

 # Cat Nip!

At five or six weeks, Mama will also start to wean us. So now is a good time for you to stock up on Mama's favorite canned and dry food.

Look out! Just like babies, we tend to make a big mess when we first start to eat solid foods. But unlike human babies, we won't be happy if you try to put a bib on us or give us a bath. Don't worry — most of the food will be landing on the floor and not on us.

Cool Cat Fact

A cat's sense of taste is better than a dog's.

Paws-ible Trouble!

Playing with our siblings is important. When we play, we learn by jumping, running, arching our backs, and hissing at each other. Mama knows this. She moves far enough away from us to get a little peace and quiet. She's also close enough that she can watch us. That way, if we start to play too rough, she can step in and stop us. I bet your own mama does that, too!

Cool Cat Fact

We can jump up to seven times our height.

Cat-ch You Later!

Now that Mama has taught us what we need to know to survive, it's your turn to take over our care. Mama will miss us a little. She may be upset for a day or two, but then she will go back to normal.

We kittens might have a harder time in our new home. We may not eat a lot for a few days. In time, though, we will be happy with you as our new mama. You just have to be patient and give us a lot of love.

Cool Cat Fact

Cats play best in even numbers. Two's company, three's a crowd.

Cat Care 101!

Your first task as our new mama is to take us to the vet. You need to make sure we have all our shots. It's also a good time to have us tested for worms. When we are about six months old, you should have your vet neuter us. That makes sure that we don't have kittens, which helps with our health and behavior, too!

Make sure to kitten-proof your home, watching out for plants or wires that could be dangerous for us. Also, you can start helping us combat any nasty fleas. We would hate to share fleas with you after you've been so good to us!

Cool Cat Fact

When you see a cat with its whiskers forward, it means that it's feeling friendly. If our whiskers are back, watch out! That's a sign that we could be feeling defensive or aggressive.

 # Cat-ch Me If You Can!

When we're new in your home, we need you to take over for our siblings as well as our mama. We are still going to want to play. We love to jump, run, stalk, and pounce. Play a game of hide-and-seek with us. Tease us with a feather toy. Give us a paper bag to rustle in.

We will love playing with you just as much as we loved playing with our brothers and sisters.

Cool Cat Fact

Cats can run up to thirty miles an hour.

Cat Nap!

Kittens are fully grown at about one year old. When we are older and on our own, we will start to sleep more regularly. We won't just fall to the floor whenever we are tired. We will still sleep a lot. Cats can sleep up to sixteen hours a day! But instead of falling to any open space on the floor, we will more likely return to a favorite place.

Cool Cat Fact

A fifteen-year-old cat has spent ten of its years sleeping.

 Purr-sonality!

We almost forgot one of your most important jobs! As our new parent, you have to give us a name. We won't be too picky. You can choose something based on how we look or act or even a name that doesn't relate to us at all. Anything will suit us. Just know that we love to hear our name being called. When you call us, especially for dinner, we'll come running!

Purr On!

There's nothing stronger than a mother's love. Mama used to tell us all the time about a stray cat named Scarlet, who bravely saved all five of her kittens from a fire. Scarlet had to go into the fire five times because she could carry out onl one kitten at a time.

We wouldn't be the cats we are today if not for our mother I bet you can say the same about your own mama. How many ways does your mother make you purr?